Glad Pam

by Tristan Horrom
illustrated by Paige Keiser

Decodable 7

McGraw Hill Education

Bothell, WA • Chicago, IL • Columbus, OH • New York, NY

MHEonline.com

Send all inquiries to:
McGraw-Hill Education
8787 Orion Place
Columbus, OH 43240

ISBN: 978-0-02-144322-2
MHID: 0-02-144322-X

Printed in China

9 10 11 12 13 DSS 28 27 26 25 24

The girl can sprint.

Pam ran past a big dog.

Pam got past the pig.
Pam trips!

Did the girl sprint past?

Pam ran and got past.

Pam did not stop.
Pam is glad!